VILLAGE
of
NORTH
CAMBRIDGESHIRE

Ian MacEachern

S.B.Publications

By the same author:–
Curiosities of Cambridgeshire (1991)

This book is dedicated to Marjory and Lyndsey

First published by S.B.Publications
c/o 19 Grove Road, Seaford, East Sussex, BN25 1TP.

ISBN 1. 85770. 020. 1

Typeset, printed and bound by Manchester Free Press.

CONTENTS

CONTENTS

ACKNOWLEDGEMENTS

In addition to Steve Benz of S.B. Publications for his enthusiasm, support and guidance, the author is indebted to the following people for their assistance in producing this book:

Mrs Peggy Day of Quy
Mr F J Ham of King's Lynn
Mr Frank Payne of Norwich
Parish Clerks of Cambridgeshire
Cambridgeshire Community Council
Cambridgeshire Federation of Women's Institutes

S.B.Publications publish a wide range of local history titles.
For details write (enclosing S.A.E.) to:–
S.B.Publications,
c/o 19 Grove Road,
Seaford,
East Sussex
BN25 1TP

INTRODUCTION

The 7th Edition of the Pocket Oxford Dictionary defines the word 'sign' as "publicly displayed symbol or device giving information". However, many of Cambridgeshire's village signs are much more than a public display of their village name, and if studied they provide a signpost to the past.

The history of village signs starts from the turn of the century, when King Edward VII was Prince of Wales. He had commissioned signs for the villages in the Sandringham Estate. The signs were carved by the Queen Alexandra Carving School located on the estate.

Prior to the Silver Jubilee of Queen Elizabeth II, only 3 village signs existed in Cambridgeshire. Balsham, erected in 1975 to commemorate the Golden Jubilee of Balsham Women's Institute, Elsworth, erected in 1975 in memory of John Throssell the Parish Clerk, and Cottenham, erected in 1976 to commemorate the Golden Jubilee of Cottenham Women's Institute. In addition, there used to be a sign in Castle Camps, which was erected to commemorate the Queen's Coronation.

However, the celebration of the Queen's Silver Jubilee in 1977 occasioned over 40 signs to be commissioned. Many of these signs and subsequent ones were made by the late Mr Harry Carter, ex-teacher at Swaffham Grammar School in Norfolk and well known signmaker. Mr Carter, who carved over 185 of the village signs in Norfolk, died in 1982. The last sign that he made for a village in Cambridgeshire was that of Great Gransden. Mr Carter occasionally worked from other people's designs but normally he did his own research and design prior to carving and painting.

Today, there are over 130 village signs, from Abbotsley to Yelling, within the county of Cambridgeshire, with many more villages planning to erect their own signs. The erection of such signs requires much research, planning and execution, which encourages and fosters a community spirit within the village.

Apart from carved oak the signs can be made from a variety of materials; for example, glass fibre, wrought iron, marine plywood or sheet steel. They can be either plain or multi-coloured, single or double-sided with the same or a different design on each side. The designs, which range from the simplistic to the intricate, portray symbolically the history of their villages, their association with agriculture and other local industries and their continuity from pre-history to the present.

Village signs are not unique to Cambridgeshire and exist in many counties throughout Britain. The counties of Norfolk and Suffolk predominate with over 350 and 200 signs each respectively. However, Cambridgeshire, which ranks third, is fast catching up and has many fine signs to offer the casual visitor. So next time you are passing through one of its villages keep a look out for the signposts to the past.

Ian J O MacEachern

NORTH CAMBRIDGESHIRE

'●' Denotes villages with signposts
(not necessarilly to scale)

North

ALCONBURY

Alconbury is situated off the A1(T) road, approximately 5 miles north-west of Huntingdon. Alconbury Brook is both forded and bridged as it winds its way through this pretty village.

In the foreground of Alconbury's village sign is depicted the old humpbacked bridge - a crossing point of the Alconbury Brook. The bridge, which is believed to date from the 15th century, is built of ashlar, square hewn blocks of stone, but has been repaired with brick parapets. Its design is interesting in that it comprises of four spans with segmental-pointed arches, chamfered on the face and with cut-water piers. The easternmost arch has been re-built and is semi-circular.

Alconbury's fine 13th-century church of St Peter and St Paul is depicted in the background of the sign. Its splendid broach spire is of note as it underwent an expensive and extraordinary restoration in 1877 when the tower but not the spire was rebuilt. The latter was propped up on massive baulks of timber while the rest was taken down and built up again. Upon completion the spire was allowed to settle down onto its new walls; fortunately it did not topple over. A brass plaque inside the church on the west wall of the nave records this remarkable feat of engineering.

BLUNTISHAM

Bluntisham village is situated 4 miles east of St Ives. The name Bluntisham literally means 'Blunt's homestead'. Thus, it is clear that there must have been a personal name Blunt in Old English for it is found in Blunsdon (Wilts.), Bluntesdon, Blunteshale (Essex), Bluntington (Worcester) and Bluntesditch in Needingworth (Ramsey Cartulary).

Bluntisham village sign, erected in August 1984 by the village Women's Institute, collapsed during the summer of 1989. It was re-erected by Harry Lee in November 1989, the woodworking having been undertaken by Deryck Steer, and stands at the junction of Hollidays and Rectory Roads. The sign depicts skating and ice hockey which took place on Bury Fen.

The origin of the name Bury was thought to have derived from the Saxon word 'burh' meaning fortified house or village, however, it almost certainly derives from the post-conquest use of 'Bury' an adjective descriptive of manor possessions. Twenty acres of this fen has belonged to the Barnfield Manor demesne since Domesday, and it was to this part of the fen that the name of Bury was first given.

Skating, or sliding, on the ice on bones and other contrivances, is a centuries old sport. True skating, however, was almost certainly popularised in England after the Restoration by the returning Royalists, who had perfected themselves in the art during their exile in Holland. It may be that the fenmen learnt to skate somewhat earlier than this from the French and Flemish refugees who settled extensively in the Fenland when driven from their homes by Spanish persecution. This argument is supported by the fact that fenmen used the word 'pattens' which is of French origin, instead of the Dutch name 'skates'. The regularity of winter floods and the ease with which spring free rivers and drains froze hard, made the Fens the best part of England for skating, and Bury Fen was perhaps the most well known, and, when well frozen, thousands of people would converge to enjoy themselves.

Also depicted on the sign is the village church of St Mary which has the unique distinction for the county of having a chancel ending in 3 sides, all of the 14th century, each of which externally terminates in a high gable rather like many churches in Brittany. The battlemented tower is topped by a tall spire visible for miles over the surrounding fenland. There used to be a curious local custom whereby a bride could free herself of all debts, incurred before her marriage, by walking across the road naked to her husband's house.

The barograph, depicted in the sign, is located inside a shelter, which was erected in memory of Charles Prentice and Mary Goodman Tebbutt by their son Louis in 1911, at the junction of the roads to Colne, Woodhurst and St Ives.

The spandrels depict apples and plums representative of fruit growing which was the greatest economic factor to have influenced the previous two generations of people in the parish.

BOTOLPH GREEN

Botolph Green is a modern development on a site that was once partially the site of the village of Botolphbridge. This village probably took the second part of its name from the presence of a bridge, as it is likely that it was the site of a crossing or ford of the river Nene from at least Roman times. Saint Botolph, who is depicted on the village sign, is a more mysterious individual, and often associated with crossings. He appears to have lived in the 7th century and his name is associated with many places locally. The Church at Thorney was renamed 'The Abbey Church of St Mary and St Botolph' after half of his body was buried there (the other half is at King Edgar's Palace, and the head at Ely).

The Botolph Green area lies to the south-west of Petersborough, beside the River Nene to the north of the Oundle Road. Originally, the site extended to either side of the road but the southern part had already been built on a number of years prior to the Botolph Green development.

One of the earliest documentary references to Botolphbridge is in the Domesday Book, which tells us that the land was held by Ranulf for King William the Conqueror. However, Botolph Bridge was never important, and as years passed it shrank (it had at different times been given as a wedding present and it is clear that the lord of the manor was often absent). Eventually the village was merged, for tax purposes, with the neighbouring village of Orton Longueville. The population declined and the church, also depicted, was finally pulled down in 1695, the stone being used in the church in Orton Longueville. The bulk of the population seems to have moved away by the 14th century, leaving the land to pasture, which is how it remained until the start of the development.

The material from the excavations at Botolphbridge can be viewed at the Peterborough City Museum, in the archaeological gallery.

BRAMPTON

There are 16 villages in England with the name of Brampton.which means 'the farm where broom grew'. Brampton in Cambridgeshire, which was mentioned in the Domesday Book, is a corruption of Brantune, a place of bramble bushes, and was probably so named by its Saxon forebears when they first settled here, because of the brambles and briars that covered the area which had to be cleared before a village could be built. Brampton's village sign, which was unveiled in 1989, depicts the bramble bush and its flower on the left-hand edge.

The sign also depicts in the background Brampton's fine medieval church of St Mary's dating back to the 14th and 15th centuries, but having a striking 'Gothic' western tower dated 1635, one of a group of 17th-century towers in the district.

Samuel Pepys, the famous 17th-century diarist, is also depicted. Pepys' House is at the entrance to Brampton near Bell End. He was not born in Brampton, but in London on 23 February 1633. He was the fifth son of a London tailor who settled in Brampton after leaving London. One of Pepys' favourite haunts was the Black Bull, a coaching inn and the oldest In Brampton; on one of the walls is an extract from his writings. In 1667, while visiting his father in Brampton, Pepys confided to his diary that 'I bless God that I am like to have such a pretty place to retire to'. However, this was not to be and he died at Clapham on 26 May 1703, aged 70, and was buried in St Olave's Church, Hart Street, London.

At the Bell End of the village there is a roundabout. On its grass verge is an 18th-century stone obelisk with hands pointing to different directions. It was dismantled during World War II in case it might give vital information to the enemy, should he have had the temerity to make a parachute landing and not know where he was. This obelisk is depicted on the sign next to Pepys.

Finally, the sign depicts Brampton Racecourse which superseded the earlier one on the Port Holme. Brampton has for many years been the centre of horse-racing and situated near the northern boundary of the parish, between Bell End and Brampton Hut and close by the Alconbury Brook is a well-appointed racecourse.

(See back cover for illustration)

5

BROUGHTON

Broughton village, which is tucked away in a secluded valley to the north of St Ives, was once the site of the manor house of the abbots of Ramsey; an extensive range of banks and mounds survives today, showing the course of the encircling moat once around the manor house.

The village sign, designed by Morag Bean and carved by Brian Dalton, was unveiled on 9 June 1984 and stands on the village green, near to the church along with the ancient brick lock-up.

The sign depicts a man and wife ploughing to denote Broughton's agricultural base. The brook and reeds denote the origin of the name Broughton, which means 'Settlement on a brook'. The setting sun in the shape of a cartwheel represents the dying craft of the local wheelwright who once flourished in the village. The Crown represents the only one of Broughton's seven public houses to remain, the Crown Inn, and the cross on the top represents the church which towers above all. The valley, within which Broughton stands, is so deep that the only evidence of its existence to the outside world is the top of the spire showing above the level of the ploughed fields which surround it on all sides.

CASTOR & AILESWORTH

The villages of Castor and Ailesworth lie 4 miles west of Peterborough. There is no visible boundary between them except for the village sign which was erected in 1982 to commemorate the Golden Jubilee, (1931-1981), of the village Women's Institute. It is a double-sided sign, which stands on the green next to Thorolds Way. One side represents Castor and the other side represents Ailesworth.

Castor is named after 'Castra' a Roman camp. Ermine Street, an old Roman road, crosses the Nene Valley in a north-westerly direction through the cornfields. The area around the road was the site of potteries where the distinctive Castor Ware was made. Many of the pots and jugs are decorated with hunting scenes in colour-coated ware. Castor must have been a very prosperous place as a magnificent praetorium was built across the top of the hill where the church now stands. Excavations have unearthed baths, fine wallplaster, mosaics and many burials. The Norman parish church is dedicated, uniquely in England, to St Kyneburga. Castor's sign, not surprisingly, is concerned with its Roman history and depicts a chariot, a piece of Castor Ware and a potter's wheel.

Ailesworth was originally a Saxon farming hamlet. Thus, the Ailesworth side depicts an agricultural scene of a ploughman and two-horse team with a sheaf of corn and a wild deer either side of this scenario. Ailesworth village green sports a magnificent horse chestnut tree, which was planted on the site of the old village pond. Thus, the double-sided sign is topped on both sides by branches of a chestnut tree. During Ailesworth's Saxon period Kyneburga and her sister, the daughters of Peada the under-king of the South Mercians 650 AD, founded a nunnery in the ruins of a Roman villa. Many artifacts including a comb, brooches, pins and domestic ware have been unearthed among traces of their humble wooden huts.

CATWORTH

Catworth, or Cateworth as it was known in the 13th century, is situated on the road from Kimbolton to Thrapston - part of the old coach road from London via St Neots to Oundle; the Wagon and Horses Inn can still be found south-west of the church. The village name literally means 'Catt's enclosure' and derives from the Old English personal name of Catt, as evidenced by other place names such as Catshall, Catsfield and Catshill.

The village sign was erected in 1977 to commemorate the Silver Jubilee of Queen Elizabeth II. The artwork on the sign depicts a ploughman with the 13th century church of St Leonard in the background. The connection between these two items is that many years ago a ploughman took his team out to plough one Sunday not knowing what day of the week it was. A local parishioner was incensed by the sight of the ploughman working on the Sabbath. However, when he discovered that the ploughman had been unaware of what day of the week it was he bequeathed a parcel of land, the rent from which was used to pay a man to ring the church bells for twenty minutes at noon every Saturday to let the villagers know that the next day would be Sunday. The field became known as Noon Leys. The bells were always rung every Saturday up until the outbreak of the Second World War, when bells were not allowed to be rung.

The carved wooden sign was made and designed by the late Mr Harry Carter of Swaffham in Norfolk. The sign stands on the green on the corner of Fox Road and High Street opposite the Race Horse public house.

9

CHATTERIS

Chatteris is recorded in the Domesday Book as Cetriz or Cietriz, both versions are thought to be Norman spellings of the Anglo-Saxon name of Ceatric, whose last syllable 'ric' is Old English for a stream. The stream referred to would have been the old Bedford Ouse, which flowed along the western boundary of Chatteris, on its route from Earith to Wisbech. This ancient Ouse, or 'West Water', supplied the first

'modern' means of communication across the swamps with Chatteris, whose 22 square miles spread east over Langwood Fen and north to Honey Hill near the Wimblington boundary. Honey Hill represents the ancient 'Huna's Island'. Huna was a devoted chaplain of St Ethelreda who, after burying her in her monastery at Ely, retired to this site. Cures were experienced at his grave, whereupon his bones were removed to Thorney. In 1810 remains of his chapel were found under Hunny Farm.

Three quarters of medieval Chatteris was Thorney's endowment, the rest supported a small abbey of nuns founded at Chatteris, circa 1006-16, by Abbot de Ramsey and his sister. The road between Chatteris and Ely, the A142, was built in 1643 when Cromwell made Henry Ireton Deputy Governor of the Isle of Ely. It was a private road with toll gates, until taken over by the County Council in 1902. Between Chatteris and Sutton the road is still called Ireton's Way.

The village sign was erected in 1977 to commemorate the Golden Jubilee of the village Women's Institute.

CHRISTCHURCH

Christchurch, 8 miles south of Wisbech in the heart of the fens, is a small village bordered on the east by the winding Old Croft River, which marks the Norfolk boundary. The course of the old Roman road, the Fen Causeway, crosses west to east just north of the village and there was an important Roman farm here. Euximoor Fen, to the north-west, in 1431 was known as Yekeswellemoor, 'marsh by cuckoo's spring or stream'. The village, prior to 1864, was part of the parish of Upwell and was known as Brimstone Hill, after the Brimstone Butterfly found there. The parish of Christchurch was created with the building of the simple red-brick, cruciform-style Christchurch, by architect John Giles, in 1864.

The village sign, carved and painted by Messrs David Turner and Godfrey Palmer respectively of March, was unveiled on 17 September 1982 by the Women's Institute and marks the occasion of the birth of Prince William of Wales. The double-sided sign features 2 different views of Christchurch, financed by the Townley family after whom the local school is named. The sheaves of corn, pitchforks and strawberry chips are representative of the area's farming interests; the surrounding fens have some of the richest and most productive soil in the country.

11

COATES

The pretty village of Coates is located on the A605 between March and Peterborough, on the northern edge of the fens, some 10 feet above the surrounding area which lies 5 feet below sea level. The village name Coates derives from the medieval English word 'cotes' the plural of 'cote', a cot; and means "a collection of cottages".

Coates has one of the largest village greens in Cambridgeshire. The main road divides it in half. North Green is surrounded by very old large lime trees, but both greens have a variety of younger trees. In the past, donkeys, horses and geese had the right to graze these greens. Consequently, on both sides of the village sign, situated on South Green, a horse, donkey and geese are depicted. The sign, designed and carved by Paul Hillard of King's Lynn, was erected in 1984 to celebrate the Diamond Jubilee of Coates Women's Institute. In the background, the village church of Holy Trinity, built of yellow brick in Norman style in 1840 by J Wild at a cost of £1563, is depicted. The church stands on the west side of North Green along with the church hall, the graveyard and the old rectory. A new rectory was built in 1987.

The reverse side depicts the Wesleyan Chapel, a severe building, also built in 1840, which stands in the centre of North Green. Some villagers objected to its building, and during one night pulled down the work of the previous day, so chapel folk guarded the construction until completion. The building was enlarged in 1866.

COLNE

Colne is a very ancient settlement and probably derives its name from the Latin word 'colonia' which means colony. Alternatively, the name could have Celtic origins deriving from a local waterway. Two fairly large Romano-British sites have been excavated within the parish and hence the village sign depicts a Roman centurion.

Much of the parish is fenland and has been from very early times. Near the Chatteris road, but some distance from the present village, was once a settlement of fen fishermen, the site of which is marked by some banks and ditches. The Anglo-Saxon village was along a former road to Somersham; an extraordinary series of double right angle bends now leads to the site of the old church of which only the ruined porch in an overgrown churchyard remains. The tower fell in 1895 ruining the building and a new church was built 3/4 of a mile to the east, where the present village is, in 1900. Stones from the old church were incorporated in the new one, which is dedicated to St Helen, the mother of the Emperor Constantine who lived during the 3rd and 4th centuries. The small green in front of St Helen's church, upon which the village sign stands, was originally the village pond but it was filled in during the late 1960s. The sign, which depicts the old church, was unveiled on the 23 July 1988 by the Parish Council on behalf of the people of Colne.

Colne has always been an agricultural village but with the arrival of the railway, fruit became an important crop and orchards were first planted between 1860 and 1880. The sign, therefore, depicts fruit orchards.

In the bottom right-hand corner a tombstone reads as follows: "The Old Church of St Helen's, which fell down in AD 1895, from the painting by E A Rogers dated 1899. Carving & Art Work by Harry Lee. Carpentry by Dereck Steer. Stonemasonary by Ted Chapman. July 1988 ".

COVENEY

Coveney and Wardy Hill are two small villages, a mile apart, set on 'islands' above the fen about 4 miles west of Ely. Coveney once stood in the bay, or cofa, of an island lake and thus means 'The island in the Bay'. Wardy Hill derives its name from 'warden's hill' or look-out. Coveney is first mentioned in 1060 when the manor was assigned for life to Elswida, one of the daughters of Oswi and Leoflada, in return for her gift to Ely Monastery of her life interest in Stetchworth; she retired here with her maidens to work at embroidery and weaving. The will is not mentioned in the Domesday Book or the Inquisitio Eliensis, and it is quite possible that this small island between the Isle of Ely proper and the Doddington island was temporarily abandoned after Elswida's death as not worth occupying.

The village sign, unveiled in July 1978 by the Coveney Women's Institute, commemorates Queen Elizabeth II's Silver Jubilee. It depicts the jewel of this small village, namely its 13th century parish church, which, like the chapel in the Tower of London, is dedicated to St Peter-ad-Vincula (St Peter in Chains), standing on a hill (as Coveney does) above a stretch of Fenland water with wildfowl flying overhead.

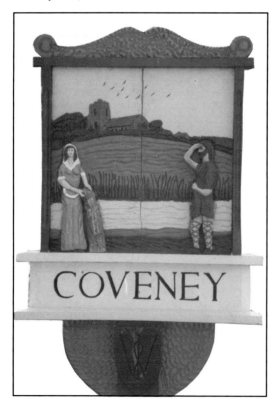

The lady on the sign represents Lady Elswida renowned for her orphreys, richly embroidered vestments, which she made for the Church and Royalty. The Saxon man on the lookout represents the hamlet of Wardy Hill (once known as Warders Hill) as it was from here that a watch was kept for cattle raiders who used to come from the direction of Chatteris.

The wooden sign, which was carved by the late Mr Harry Carter of Swaffham in Norfolk, stands near to Coveney Pound, dated 1840, which was used to impound cattle that had strayed from the common grazing areas.

DEEPING GATE

Like Borough Fen, Deeping Gate is a civil parish with no recognisable village, no church, and only a small population. It stands between Maxey and Northborough and extends up to the river Welland covering the two bridges over to the Deepings. The hamlet has been associated with Maxey from earliest recorded times and is served by Maxey church. The Fairfax family owned a house here in the 14th century. The word 'Gate' in a place-name means 'an entry'. Thus, the origins of the parish of Deeping Gate probably lie in the fact that it was once an enlarged bridge-head which guarded the two ways into Deeping.

Deeping Gate sign was made by Mr Ray Ellison of Maxey. The sign's design is based on 3 panels displaying agricultural and wildlife scenes with the centre panel declaring Deeping Gate as the 'Gateway To the Deepings'.

GATEWAY TO THE DEEPINGS

DEEPING GATE

DODDINGTON

'There are immense marshes, now a black pool of water, now a foul running stream, and also many islands...' so wrote an 8th century monk of the area. Doddington is situated on one of those islands. Its name derives from 'farm of Dodda's people'. By the Middle Ages, Doddington had become one of the most important places in the Isle of Ely, and it steadily grew in stature until its original parish became the largest in Cambridgeshire, and one of the largest in England, and covered 37,801 acres including the hamlets of March, Wimblington and Benwick.

Doddington's village sign, unveiled on Saturday 28 April 1984, marks the Diamond Jubilee of the village Women's Institute. Designed and carved by Len Hopkins, it stands on a small green, at the junction of Newgate Street and Church Lane, known as Policeman's Corner. It consists of two different carved wooden shields, fashioned from the hard wood iroko, similar to mahogany, mounted either side of an oak post. Each shield is divided into halves by a diagonal band of yellow, which together form a symbolic 'Primrose Hill'.

The left-hand shield depicts a Bishops Mitre and 4 crosses representative of Doddington as a Manor of the Bishops of Ely, from the 12th to 17th century, which encompassed the parochial chapeltries of March, Benwick and Wimblington. Below the yellow diagonal woodland is depicted where deer used to be hunted by the Doddington 'Buckhounds' led by the Lord of the Manor. This woodland subsequently fell to the plough and nearby Turf Fen obtained its name from the local turf diggings for fuel, which are represented by the now obsolete 'Spade and Beckett'.

The top half of the right-hand shield depicts three of the remaining notable features of the village, namely the 18th century 'Moat House', the 'Post Mill' and the 'Round House'. The Round House, built in the days of mud and wattle, was partly demolished in 1949 and a new section built onto its rear. However, when viewed from the front, the original round house shape and thatched roof can still be seen. Below the diagonal the symbols of two families who have figured prominently in the history of the village are depicted. The Harding's Arms are displayed to commemorate their ardent patronage to the benefit of the village community.

The Tower of London and the Fleur-de-Lis represent the Peyton family, the first Lords of the Manor after the Bishops of Ely. When Heton was appointed Bishop the manorial rights were already on lease to Sir John Peyton, and they were granted to him outright in 1602. The manor continued in the Peyton family until the end of the 19th century.

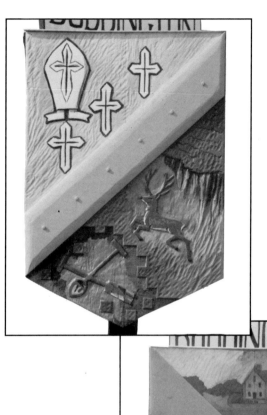

DOWNHAM–IN–THE–ISLE OR LITTLE DOWNHAM

Downham, whose name means 'estate on a hill' has, since the 14th century, been called Downham–in–the–Isle or Little Downham to distinguish it from Downham Market, Norfolk. It is situated at the northern edge of the Isle of Ely proper; from here the road west to Pymore drops steeply, and at Tower Farm, where the remains of Downham palace are to be found, Wisbech, 15 miles away, can be seen on a clear day, and to the south, Ely.

The village sign was unveiled on the 5 June 1977 and commemorates the Queen's Silver Jubilee, 1952-77. The double-sided sign, designed by Edward E Taylor of Little Downham and made by H & K Mabbett of Colchester, stands on the rising ground of Church Green not far from the Norman church of St Leonard. On the front of the sign, the left-hand Coat of Arms is of The Isle of Ely. The Central Arms are of the historic Lord of the Manor, The Bishop of Ely, and the right–hand Devise is of Bishop of Alock, Bishop of Ely, 1486-1500, who rebuilt the Palace of Downham. Bishop Alcock was a discriminating builder and, as Master of the Rolls, one of the most important judges in the country. He also founded Jesus College in Cambridge. A chapel in Ely Cathedral is dedicated to his memory. Also carved in relief, but not coloured, are reed mace symbolising the swampy fenland, and oak leaves representing the bog oaks.

On the reverse side, the left-hand Coat of Arms is of Bishop Lancelot Andrewes, Bishop of Ely 1609-1619 and co-translator of the Authorised Version of the Bible, who was responsible for translating from Genesis to the Second Book of Kings; he is said to have known 14 different languages.

The Arms depict an open Bible with the following words on the left and right-hand pages respectively:

PSALM 132 V 14
This is my rest for ever;
here will I dwell
for I have desired it.

PSALM 133 V 1
Behold how good
and how pleasant it
is for brethren to
dwell together in unity!

In the centre is a water-draining windmill, one of the 700 in the fenland introduced by the remarkable Dutch engineer Cornelius Vermuyden during the drainage of the fens between 1630-1652. The right-hand Devise is of Abbot Leonard 559 AD, patron saint of prisoners, to whom the parish church is dedicated. Also shown is the emblem of Little Downham Women's Institute, founded April 1918, being the first branch in the Isle of Ely.

The name Downham–in–the–Isle is carved in versal letters used by medieval scribes and comes from an early name of the village recorded in 970 when the Manor of Dounham was given to the Monks of Ely. Dounham derives from the Anglo-Saxon words 'dun', meaning a down or hill, and 'ham', meaning an enclosure.

19

DOWNHAM
IN·THE·ISLE

DOWNHAM
IN·THE·ISLE

EARITH

Earith, whose name derives from 'hithe' meaning an 'inland port' (though a muddy one as the Anglo-Saxon word 'ear' means 'mud'), was probably an important landing place for merchandise before the River Ouse was short circuited in the 17th century.

Just below the church of St Mary lie Bury and Little Fens, a scene of many memorable skating races and the birthplace of the game Bandy (a game similar to ice hockey). Thus, Earith sign depicts figures skating on frozen ice.

In 1130 William of Malmesbury wrote of the Fens:

'Here is such plenty of fish as to cause astonishment in strangers while natives laugh at their surprise; waterfowl are so plentiful that five persons may eat to satiety for a penny.'

In medieval times fresh meat was always scarce in winter time, besides being forbidden on Fridays; and sea fish were only obtainable in the form of salted herrings. Freshwater fish, therefore, played an important part in most people's diet. Fishing, however, was not free to all. The whole length of the Ouse, for example, where it was practicable to net fish, was divided up into fisheries, belonging to various Lords of Manors who considered them valuable possessions. The exclusive right of fishing at Earith was still exercised about 60 years ago by members of the Ayres family. Earith's fishing past is represented on the village sign by four freshwater fish.

The eel was probably the most important fish in fenland diet and the annual capture of hundreds of thousands is recorded in the Cambridgeshire portion of the Domesday Survey. Thus, an eel is depicted either side of the name 'Earith'.

Finally, depicted above the skating figures are three wildfowl. Wildfowling never assumed the same importance as fishing in Earith owing to the relatively small amount of fenland that was permanently flooded, and the absence of a suitable pond or mere where a duck decoy could be worked. For wildfowling, Earith fishermen used a special type of boat, a punt, which was flat bottomed and pointed at each end. They were known as 'gunning punts', because they were fitted with a heavy flintlock, and were pushed along by a pole called a 'spread'. These punts required considerable skill to manoeuvre within range of wary fowl. However, one lucky shot could bring in as much as a labourer could earn in a fortnight, but the dangers of 'bursting guns (many of the guns were family heirlooms, and were consistently overcharged) and death from pneumonia following upsets in ice-cold water, were always a fair risk. Such was the skill of the Earith wildfowler, that they became known by the local nickname of 'Earith Gunners'.

EASTON

The name Easton literally means 'East Farm' and was so named to distinguish it from Old Weston (West Farm) on the other side of the Hundred-centre at Leighton. It is a secluded village which stands about half a mile to the south of the road from Huntingdon to Thrapston and six–and–a–half miles from the former town.

Designed by Linda Ramsey and carved and painted by Glyn Mould, the village sign, which was unveiled on Sunday 5 November 1989, stands on the grass verge of Church Road, opposite the church. It depicts the village centre with its stream, thatched cottages and church spire in the background. The church, which dates from the 12th century, has a fine 15th–century oak screen under the chancel arch, of five bays with open tracery above and traceried panels below; the coving and loft have gone and the remaining portion is somewhat mutilated, however, the rood-loft staircase remains intact on the south side. It is said that many years ago village girls who had contravened the moral law were placed in the staircase for a week - locked in, so that they were unable to sit, stand or lie down though they were fed.

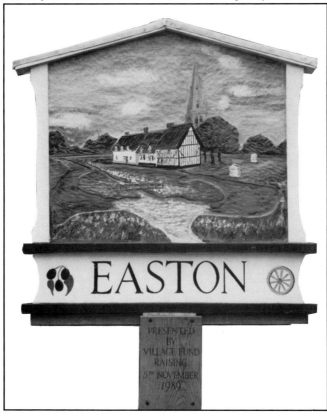

ELM

The village name was recorded as eolum in 973, so it is possible that Elm was a place for 'eels' rather than 'elms', which are depicted on the village sign. They would have teemed when all the Midland rivers rushed past Elm to get to the Wash at Wisbech.

Designed and carved by the late Mr Harry Carter of Swaffham, the village sign, which was erected in 1981, is sited on the grass verge between Fridaybridge Road and Birch Grove, almost opposite the Parish cemetery. The artwork on the sign depicts the magnificent 13th–century church of All Saints, around which the village is centred. The west tower is the earliest and finest part of the church, with its broad storeys of lancet arcading, similar to that of West Walton in Norfolk.

There was great parochial unrest when proposals were made to lay a tram-line through the village in 1881, a petition was sent to Parliament. The tramway was laid from Wisbech to Upwell alongside the canal. Neither have survived, the tramway was a victim of Dr Beeching's cuts and the canal was filled in when the Anglian Water Authority rerouted the drainage in the fens. Thus, the village sign depicts a bridge over the old River Leam, the drainage canal, which was situated near the present site of the Church Hall. Finally, the spandrels depict sheep as many years ago the area was mainly devoted to sheep rearing.

ELTON

Elton is a very pretty village, which lies close to the River Nene at the western boundary of the parish, near to the border of Cambridgeshire and Northamptonshire. In the 10th century, the village was recorded as Aethelington. Therefore, the village name probably derives from the Anglo-Saxon personal name of Aethel and a literal translation would be 'Aethel's farm'.

Designed and made by Glyn Mould of Lilford Park near Oundle, Elton village sign, which stands at the junction of Vinco Terrace and Overend, was erected in 1983 to celebrate the 50th Anniversary of the Women's Institute. The top of the sign depicts some of Elton's many fine buildings.

The central picture of the village sign is the Sapcote tower of Elton Hall, a romantic Gothic house, originally built by the Sapcote family, which has been the ancestral home of the Proby family for over 300 years. It stands in the midst of unspoilt landscaped parkland, on a site where there has been a house since the Norman Conquest. Sir Peter Proby, Lord Mayor of London and Comptroller of the Royal Household, was granted land and property at Elton by Queen Elizabeth I. His grandson, Sir Thomas Proby, completed the main house in 1666 incorporating the medieval chapel and gatehouse. In the 18th century John Proby was created the 1st Earl of Carysfort in recognition of his services as a politician and diplomat. He and his successors enlarged the house and gave it the 18th century character that it has today. Both the gatehouse and the vaulted crypt are built of Barnack stone and original. The exterior is decorated with mouldings of the Sapcote crest and has a distinct embattled parapet on its great tower, which once had portcullis.

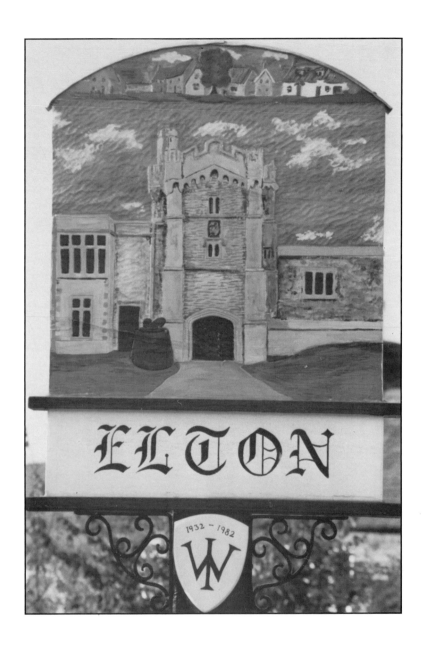

ETTON

Etton stands serenely in the midst of perfectly flat reclaimed fenland like an island in a sea. Daniel Defoe, the journalist and novelist whose best-known work, Robinson Crusoe, appeared in 1719, is associated with Etton. His parents lived here before moving to London, Daniel's birthplace. The church of St Stephen's at Etton is a fine example of an Early English church to the east of which is an Elizabethan manor house which is featured on the village sign.

Etton village sign, which stands on the small green off Rectory Lane, was designed by the late Mr Len Vergette, a local farmer and former Chairman of the Parish Council, carved by Mr Ellison of Maxey and erected by Mr Walter Henfrey. It depicts the old Manor House in the background with corn, mice and berries in the foreground as portrayal of the pretty countryside in which Etton is located.

EYE

There are several places called 'Eye', which derives from the Old English word "eg" (pronounced "eeg"), and the name means the same in each case - "water", "or a place surrounded by water". The village was first settled on a gravel ridge in the midst of the fen and this has shaped the village of today with its long main street. It has little of interest to see as it was almost completely destroyed in a fire on 28 November 1848.

Sited in the yard of St Matthew's church, which escaped the 1848 fire, is Eye's double-sided village sign, which was erected in 1978 and commemorates Queen Elizabeth II's Silver Jubilee. On the one side is a picture of the Village Crier; the last one died during the 1930s and he used to inform the villagers when farmers required pea pickers etc. The other side portrays Hereward the Wake and his wife because of the alleged connection with the village. There is tradition to the effect that Hereward once owned land at Eye, but this is hard to authenticate historically. However, there is no doubt about the existence of Hereward as a person. It is known that he harried the Normans, that he was probably the hero of the insurgents' stronghold at Ely and that he appears in the Domesday Book as a holder of lands, under Norman lords, in the counties of Worcester and Warwick.

GLATTON

The name of Glatton means 'cheerful' or 'pleasant village', a reputation it has held for over 1200 years. It is a pretty village, well-treed and with numerous old houses of distinction, which surrounds a four-sided figure formed by roads.

Glatton village sign, which stands on the corner of Glatton Ways and High Haden Road, was erected by the village council in 1973 to commemorate Queen Elizabeth II's Silver Jubilee. The sign depicts the old cottage of Allways, as typical of many thatched cottages in the village, and the fine parish church of St Nicholas, which originates from the late 12th century. Inside, fixed on the west wall, is a strange carved head, found in the churchyard, probably Roman. It appears to have been placed upside down. It is said that it represents the Medusa as it has long hair which with some stretch of the imagination could look like snakes.

GLINTON

Glinton village is situated six miles north–east of Peterborough, just off the A15. The village sign, which was unveiled during October 1979 to commemorate the Silver Jubilee of Queen Elizabeth II, is located at the central crossroads of the village, off Helpston Road, and depicts the two main elements of village life.

The first is the 12th–century parish church of St Benedict which was originally a

chapel of ease to the parish of Peakirk. Its gargoyles are an interesting feature. One cannot fail to notice that of those on the south side, three show faces and the fourth the opposite. The story is told that when the stonemason failed to obtain his remuneration he completed the work in an appropriate manner.

The second theme of the village sign is that of agriculture, which surrounds the village. The sign depicts the figure of a man engaged in ploughing with a two–horse team.

GREAT GIDDING

Great Gidding is the largest and oldest of the three Giddings and shares with Yelling the distinction of being one of the two oldest villages in the county. In 1549 the village name was recorded as Great Gedyng, which derives from the personal name of Gydel, and a sensible translation would be 'Gydel's people'. The 'Great' derives from Gidding Prioris, so called from the holding of the Prior of Huntingdon. The village stands in one of the remotest parts of the county set in very rural and unspoilt country. It straddles the B660 Kimbolton to Ramsey road.

Great Gidding village sign, which stands on the green at the junction of Winwick Road, Main Street and Chapel End, was erected in March 1987 with monies received from parishioners and local organisations, such as the Women's Institute. It does not commemorate any particular event. It depicts St Michael's church, which dates from the 13th century, and the old windmill, long since disused.

GREAT STAUGHTON

Great Staughton, whose name translates as 'farm enclosure made of stumps or stocks', is half a mile from the Bedfordshire border and straddles the main road from St Neots to Kimbolton, the A45. The village street here has been known since the 16th century as Staughton Highway. At its eastern end the road crosses the River Kym by a bridge which was in the early 16th century called the Wrong Bridge.

The village sign, which was carved by Mr Glyn Mould of Lilford Craft Workshops near Oundle, was presented to the village in 1985 by the Great Staughton Horticultural Society. In the foreground a farm worker is depicted ploughing his field with horse and plough representative of Staughton's long association with agriculture. In the middleground the River Kym is depicted.

The oldest part of the village, Church End, is centred around the Church of St. Andrew and Place House, part of a former mansion, about a third of a mile to the west of the Highway on a bye-road to Pertenhall. The River Kym is again crossed here by a bridge called Staughton Bridge in 1509. The large 800–year–old church, which is featured on the sign, has a very fine western tower of Northamptonshire type built about 1526.

The remaining object depicted, in the top right-hand corner of the sign, is Staughton's Prayer or Preaching Cross, which is situated, almost opposite the sign itself, on the north side of Staughton Highway. It consists of a base of modern brickwork supporting a tone octagonal shaft upon which is a cube with a panel bearing the inscription '1637, E.I.' on the north side and a sundial on the south, the whole being surmounted by a sphere.

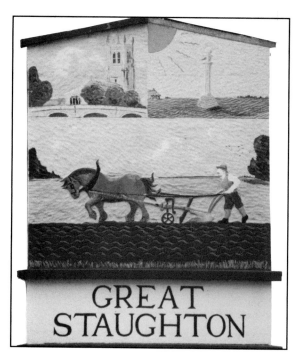

GUYHIRN

Guyhirn, near Wisbech and 4 miles from Parson Drove, is a one-sided village developed at the side of the lofty banks of the river Nene. The village name derives from the Anglo-Saxon word 'hyrne', meaning 'a corner, nook or hiding place', and from the Norman personal name of Guy. The Ramsey Chartulary mentions 20 men of name Guy. Thus, a literal translation is 'Guy's retreat'.

The village sign was unveiled on 8 June 1977 by Guyhirn Women's Institute. the sign depicts the 1660 Guyhirn Puritan Chapel of Ease. This chapel may well have begun as a Meeting House for break-away Huguenot/Walloon refugee families formerly of Thorney colony dissatisfied with the 'popish practices' of Thorney Abbey. The small building is an almost unique Puritan chapel. The chapel has a small bell in its turret bearing the initials W.W., possibly those of a church warden or donor, and the date 1637.

HADDENHAM

Haddenham, whose name derives from the Anglo-Saxon name of Heada and literally means 'Heada's home', is the highest, at 116 feet above sea level, and the most southern village in the Isle of Ely.

Designed and made by locals John Sheffield and Mr Hauxwell, Haddenham's double-sided village sign was erected on the village green in April 1983 and donated to the village by the Friends of Haddenham. On the one side, in the foreground, is the river - the Old West - sweeping through the Fen to the hill on which Haddenham is built. In the middleground a man is shown ploughing with a two–horse team along with a farm worker with a sheaf of corn representative of the role that agriculture plays in the life of the village. In the background, landmarks such as the watertower and 13th–century parish church of the Holy Trinity are depicted.

The reverse side shows another agricultural scene with fruit orchards and farm animals. In the background a mill is depicted representative of the various mills that the village used to have. The remains of the last mill in the village can be found, about 1/4 mile to the south, on the minor road to the small hamlet of Aldreth.

(See Title page for illustration of village sign).

HADDON

Haddon is a remote village in farming country 8 miles south–west of Peterborough, and is one of a series of small settlements along a trackway commencing at Sawtry and ending at Chesterton. The village, whose name derives from the Old English words 'haed-dun' meaning 'heath covered hill', comprises of a few cottages, a farmhouse and the rectory clustered around the small Early- English church.

Haddon village sign is rather primitive in design being a nameboard set in wrought iron surmounting the 'Old Village Well'.

HARTFORD

Hartford, once a small and pleasant riverside village about a mile and a half from Huntingdon, has now been absorbed into the ever expanding borough of Huntingdon. It is the earliest settlement of this stretch of the river Ouse, older than nearby Godmanchester. The place name has over the years been misinterpreted and has nothing to do with 'harts' or 'stags'. The letter 't' was not in the name a century ago and in the 17th century the name was Herford. The Domesday Book recorded the settlement as 'Hereforde' literally meaning 'army ford'. By the church, which stands on the extreme edge of the river bank, the fordway can still be seen.

The sign depicts the 12th–century parish church of All Saints. It also depicts a cottage facing the river. This cottage was originally the Anchor Inn and in 1275 a waterwheel was constructed there.

HOUGHTON & WYTON

Houghton & Wyton are adjoining picturesque villages situated, on the north bank of the Ouse, some 2 to 3 miles west of St Ives and midway between St Ives and Huntingdon. The names of both villages are Anglo-Saxon in form with Houghton being the older. Its first recording in history is in the 10th–century Ramsey Abbey records where is it spelt HOUTTON. The Domesday Book of 1086 records it as HOCTUNE. Variations of the 13th–century include HOCTON in 1207, HOHTUN in 1253 and HOUTON in 1279. The village name means 'the farm (TUN or TON) at the foot of the hill (HOH or HOUGH). Manor Farm is the successor of the original 'TON' and Houghton Hill is the hill below which it stands. Wyton is a later Saxon name of a type somewhat more difficult to translate and experts differ as to what it really means. In the early Ramsey Abbey records, and in the Domesday Book, it appears as WITUNE. Later derivatives include WICTUN and WITTON, the latter which survived until the mid-19th–century. The meaning is thought to be 'the farm near another farm'.

Carved by Harry Lee with carpentry by Derek Steer, the village sign was unveiled on 9 July 1989. It portrays Houghton Mill, the 14th–century church of St Mary, the village clock, Wyton Church and a Blenheim Bomber.

Houghton Water Corn Mill, which is found at the end of Church Lane, belongs to the National Trust. It is one of the last and most complete to survive along the course of the river Ouse. There have been mills on the site for at least a thousand years but much of the present mill dates from the 17th–century when it replaced an earlier one destroyed by fire.

Near the centre of the village Green stands a picturesque thatched shelter, given in 1902 in memory of G W Brown. On top of this thatch is the village clock depicted on the sign.

Unlike other riverside village churches, Wyton's church of St Margaret and All Saints is not built on the river bank and it is very probable the village is much later in origin that the others along the Ouse and has been 'tucked in' close to Houghton, so close indeed, that it is almost impossible to state where one village begins and the other ends.

Near to Wyton is RAF Wyton, the first of seven service airfields in the county whose airfield was established towards the end of the First World War. The land was sold off for agricultural purposes in 1918, but reopened in 1936. It greatly increased in size during World War II. RAF Wyton had the task of sending out a Blenheim bomber in September 1939, only hours after the outbreak of war, to make a reconnaissance flight over German ports. This was the first British operational sortie of the war. Thus, to commemorate this significant event the village sign depicts a Blenheim Bomber.

LEVERINGTON

Two miles north–west of Wisbech is the village of Leverington, whose name derives from 'the farm of Leofhere's people'. The village sign, which was unveiled on Sunday 26 March 1978 to commemorate Queen Elizabeth II's Silver Jubilee, stands on the triangle of grass at the junction of Perry Road and Church End. It depicts Leverington Church, along with the symbols of St Leonard, the patron saint of prisoners, a shovel and handcuffs.

St Leonard's 13th-century church, perhaps the most graceful in the county, is a prominent landmark with its beautiful tall steeple, set into a Norman turret with four smaller turrets to support it.

LITTLEPORT

Littleport is a large parish on the eastern border of the Isle, 5 miles north of Ely. The derivation of the name Littleport may be exactly what it says, a small portus, or harbour, up to which boats or barges could once sail. However, legend has it that King Canute founded this fishing village on the Ouse and named it Littleport. Alternatively, the name may have derived from a walled market-town with a porta, or fortified gate, somewhat similar to the Ely Porta.

Littleport village sign, researched by Mrs Maureen Scot and designed and made by Mr Paul Hillard of King's Lynn in Norfolk, was unveiled 6 April 1984 by members of Littleport Women's Institute in commemoration of their Diamond Jubilee, 1922-1982, and stands on a small triangular green at the intersection of Pont's Hill and the A1101, Wisbech Road.

The front side depicts the Bread Riots of 1816. A man is shown standing on a bench speaking to a group of rowdy supporters with The Globe public house, at which the men used to meet, in the background. The defeat of Napoleon in 1815 left the country impoverished; agricultural labourers earned only 8/- or 9/- a week, and those unemployed almost starved. On 22 May 1816, fifty or sixty men were in The Globe discussing disturbances which had already taken place elsewhere. A mob sallied forth to sack a number of houses and shops, and on the following day, armed with simple farm implements and preceded by a wagon bearing fen punt guns, attacked premises in Ely. The riots were suppressed by cavalry, and between 70 and 80 persons were arrested. Five men were subsequently hanged at Ely and 25 others transported to Botany Bay. Apparently, no one would lend a cart to take the condemned men to the gallows so one had to be hired elsewhere at a cost of five guineas. High on the wall at the rear of St Mary's Church in Ely, the Littleport Rioters' Memorial records the shameful murder of these 5 men hanged by the Bishop of Ely, as an example of his absolute authority. The Fen tigers never forgave nor forgot, and countless German mercenaries, who had been called in to track down the luckless men, vanished mysteriously in the fog-enshrouded dykes and rivers.

Archaeological evidence suggests that the Romans were responsible for the earliest attempts at drainage in this area. Thus, below the main panel of the sign is a shield with a Roman head on it, representative of the early Roman occupation of the area. In the background, the reverse side depicts the 14th–century church of St George, which was almost entirely rebuilt late in the 15th century and then restored in 1857. The yacht and cruiser on the River Ouse represent Littleport's modern marina which replaced the old cargo port which used to provide dock and warehouse facilities for barges from King's Lynn. The L.N.E.R. steam train engine represents Littleport's rail connection; its station lies on the Ely-Lynn branch of the Eastern Region, British Railways, which was opened in 1847. The windmill is representative of the various mills that used to exist in the surrounding area. Finally, in the foreground, a man fishing represents the excellent angling to be afforded on the river. The shield, below the main panel, bears the crest of Littleport College.

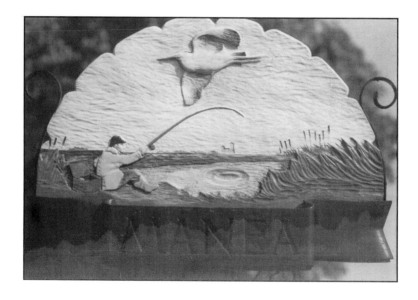

MANEA

Manea, whose name derives from 'island held in common', is a village whose past and present is almost wholly involved in agriculture.

The double-sided village sign, designed and carved by B T Winch, stands in Station Road opposite the school. It was presented to the village by the Manea Floral Club and unveiled on the 29th July 1981 to commemorate the village winning the Best Kept Village Competition. On the one side, representative of the village's long association with agriculture, is depicted a farmer ploughing with a two-horse team, and on the other side the Washes are depicted with an angler, as fishing is prominent in the village.

Manea was a hamlet of Coveney until the cutting of the Old and New Bedford rivers in the 17th century made them 16 miles apart by road. Between these two rivers is the great strip of regularly flooded grazing marshland known as the Washland upon which immense numbers of wildfowl, including the rare ruff, the black-tailed godwit and occasionally the black tern, over winter. Thus, above the angler, the sign depicts a bird in flight.

MARCH --PEAS HILL GREEN

Peas Hills Green is an exclusive village green development, by AB Homes, situated on the western outskirts of March, whose name derives from the Old English word 'mearc' meaning 'boundary', which is appropriate as March was originally a hamlet of Doddington. The Peas Hill sign, was designed by architect Andrew Allen of Allen Brothers, the developers whose initials are displayed on the spandrels, and made by Mr Paul Hillard of King's Lynn. It depicts a Roman helmet and spear representative of the fact that March was once the site of a Roman settlement.

The town of March probably owes its origin to the ford on the old course of the Nene river where the road between Ely and Wisbech, the two chief towns of the Isle, crossed the river. Hence the village sign symbolically depicts the Nene river.

MAXEY

Maxey village is spread east and west along a straight road with Stepping Lane on the north running parallel and close to it. At Castle End a large rectangular moat and some subsidiary ditches mark the site of where Maxey 'Castle' once stood. Although now disappeared, the castle must have been of some size and importance for here once lived the Countess of Richmond, Margaret Beaufort, who was mother of Henry VII and Lady of the Manor.

Carved by Ray Ellison, Maxey's village sign, which commemorates the Royal Wedding, stands on a small green off School Lane. It depicts the family crests of De La Mare, Beaufort and De Torpel on the left, and the broad grey church of St Peter on the right, which stands isolated at a crossroads nearly a mile west of the village. The Coats of Arms are depicted because of the associations of the families with the village. Beaufort has already been mentioned. De Torpel and De La Mare were knights who once patrolled the area around Maxey. De Torpel patrolled between Ufford and Maxey; whereas De La Mare patrolled the Helpstone area. The sign itself is in the

shape of a heraldic shield with what is known as a 'bend' from top left to right, which separates the depicted shields and church. The 'bend' symbolically represents the furrows of a ploughed field, which together with the horse and ploughman represent the village's close association with agriculture.

MEPAL

Mepal, whose name derives from 'Meapa's nook', is a small agricultural fenland village lying approximately half a mile off the Fen Trunk Road between Chatteris and Ely, which straddles the Bedford Rivers.

Designed from a postcard of the early 1900s and made by Paul Hillard of King's Lynn, Mepal's village sign, which was unveiled by its Women's Institute to commemorate their Diamond Jubilee on 8 March 1983, stands on a small green in the centre of the village opposite the Village Hall. The design incorporates the original Vermuyden timber trestle bridge over the New Bedford (or Hundred Foot) River, which was removed, leaving only the footings, when the present reinforced concrete bridge and viaduct were built.

The sign also shows the loading of sheep from the nearby washlands into typical flat barges which were then used for transport of livestock and farm produce. A haywain passing over the bridge shows another aspect of fen life. The background of old buildings, many still standing today, completes the scene.

MURROW

Murrow, 14 miles north-east of Peterborough, straddles the B1187 between Parson Drove and Guyhirn. The original settlement dates back to Roman times and existed on high ground, known as Fendyke Bank, where a road and row of houses were built, long before the drainage of the fens. Its name means 'row of homes in the marsh'. In the first half of this century, the village was almost entirely inhabited by railway and land workers and Murrow was noted for its two railway stations and famous for its one of only two 'diamond crossings', where the London & North Eastern, March-Spalding, line crossed that of the Midland & Great Northern, Wisbech-Peterborough, track.

Designed by Mr Les Pooley of Wisbech St Mary and made by Mr Rodney Cranwell of Stow Bridge, Murrow's village sign, which was unveiled on 16 October 1976 to commemorate the Golden Jubilee of Murrow Women's Institute, stands on the Bank near to the village school. It depicts the famous 'diamond' railway crossing with a steam locomotive in the centre, the Women's Institute monogram and the dates of their 50th anniversary, 1926-1976.

NEWBOROUGH

The original Borough Fen, several thousand acres of marshland and fen, occupied nearly half of the eastern end of the former Soke of Peterborough. The land was eventually drained, culminating in enclosure in 1822 and the formation of the fields and the long straight narrow drove roads that one sees today. Part of this operation included the making of a long 'enclosure' road, some seven and a half miles in length, from Thorney to Peakirk, which divided the fen into two. That part to the north retained its original name and became a civil parish. Most of the land to the south was constituted into a separate ecclesiastical parish named Newborough in 1823. Another straight 'enclosure' road running from Eardley Grange in the north to Gunton and Dogsthorpe in the south crossed the Thorney to Peakirk road at right-angles approximately half-way along and here, south of the crossroads, was built the present small village to accommodate the farmers and smallholders displaced by the process of enclosure and to house newcomers.

Carved by Mr Ray Ellison of Maxey, the village sign, which was erected on 2 July 1988 by the village Women's Institute, stands in the centre of the village. The sign depicts an agricultural scene, as the area comprises mainly of a few large farms. The sign also depicts the Parish Church of St Bartholomew which was erected in 1821 in 'Churchwarden-Gothic' style and paid for by selling land in Borough Fen. Finally the sign depicts a duck representative of the nearby Duck Decoy, the gem of Borough Fen. The earliest reference is in 1670, when the Decoyman (Mr Williams) was granted permission to pierce the river Welland to lead water to his decoy pond. The Decoy was continuously managed by the Williams family until the death of Billy Williams in 1958, who was well known in the district. In 1951 the Wildfowl Trust undertook the financial responsibility of ringing the ducks that are caught, instead of killing them, and the decoy is the oldest of the few decoys that survive today.

NEWTON IN THE ISLE

Newton in the Isle is a small village situated in the north of the county, bordering Lincolnshire and Norfolk, on the B1165 some 4 miles from Wisbech, lying just west of the 'Roman Bank'. Like Leverington, Tydd and other parishes on the 'north side', Newton was protected from the sea by this ancient sea bank.

Geoffrey de Marisco was the last in the male line of the Mariscos who held the manor at Newton. His daughter, Desiree, by her marriage to Sir Roger Colvile of Carlton Colvile (Suffolk) brought the manor to the family which was so prominently associated with Newton until the end of the 18th century. Sir John Colvile III, was perhaps the most remarkable of the family. In 1409 he was sent by Henry IV on an important mission to Italy, and at the end of the following year he was appointed Constable of Wisbech Castle, a position he held until at least 1446. In 1412 he accompanied an expedition to France against the Duke of Orleans, and the following year commanded a naval force which won a victory over the French in the English Channel. He also fought at Agincourt, and for these and other services was granted a pension of £40 a year for life with which he founded and endowed the College, which stood on the old Roman Bank near to the old rectory, and Chantry (the Chapel of St Mary in the Marsh or "Capella Maris") in 1403. The endowment was used to maintain 4 chaplains, 4 clerks and 10 poor men. The poor lived in the building called the Bede House and were given 6 pence per week and clothing.

The village sign, which was unveiled in September 1976, was commissioned by the Newton Society and made by the late Mr Harry Carter of Swaffham. It depicts Sir John Colvile III and the College. The White Lion Rampant, depicted on the sign post, is from the Colvile coat of arms which has displayed a white lion since AD 1280.

At the top of the sign, six bells are depicted, which are representative of the six bells of St James Church, built in the 13th century, which has a rare rood loft gallery. To the left of the bells, a woad plant is depicted. Woad was grown locally until the end of the 19th century and probably processed in the Woad Mill at Parson Drove. One of Newton's public houses is called The Woadman's Arms and another is known as The White Lion with a Lion rampant as its sign. The apples and strawberries in the spandrels represent the fruit growing industry.

NORTHBOROUGH

The village of Northborough is situated on the A15, seven miles north of Peterborough. Northborough was first mentioned in the 12th century Survey of Northamptonshire. The village sign, which is another carved by Mr Ray Ellison of Maxey, is located on the verge of a layby off the main road through the village, and depicts the parish church of St Andrew. Small and towerless, it is the last resting place of two people closely connected with Oliver Cromwell; his widow and John Claypole, his second daughter Elizabeth's husband. Elizabeth, who is said to have interceded for Royalist prisoners, died at the early age of 29 in 1658, the year of her father's death, and was buried in Westminster Abbey. Her remains were treated with more respect than those of her father, which were disinterred and hung on the gallows at Tyburn in 1661. John Claypole married Elizabeth in 1646, the year he raised a troop of horse and became master of the horse to his father-in-law, the Protector, and one of his peers. Imprisoned as a suspect in 1678, he survived another 10 years, dying in 1688, thirty years after Elizabeth and her father. John Claypole's manor house, whose 14th

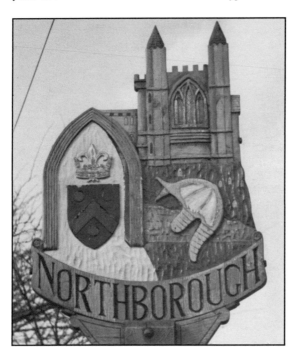

century structure was greatly altered 3 centuries later, still stands in Northborough. It is believed that the house was originally built by the De La Mare family. The family crest of Claypole, which is also the school badge, is depicted on the sign, as is a 'Cromwellian' style hat. The Royal crown is representative of the fact that Royalty once stayed at Northborough Manor, or Northborough Castle as it is known today.

ORTON LONGUEVILLE

There are two Ortons, about a mile apart, built along cul-de-sacs running southward from the main Alwalton to Peterborough road. Orton is an abbreviation of Overton which means 'the village on the river bank'. Thus, Orton Longueville village once belonged to the Longueville family of Norman origin.

The village sign was erected in 1975 by the village Women's Institute to commemorate the European Architectural Heritage Year. The sign depicts Henry de Longueville of Normandy, the first member of the family, of whom there is any record, who held the manor in 1166, and his wife standing in the old doorway of Orton Hall, which still stands in the village. The Hall, house of the Gordons, Marquesses of Huntly and Earls of Aboyne, dates from the 16th century. It is built of the famous Barnack ragstone from the nearby Barnack quarry, whose stone was also quarried to build the church and many of the village houses. The hall, which was extended in 1855 is today a girls school. Its avenue is flanked by magnificent Wellingtonia trees. Henry de Longueville's wife is reputed to have been a relative of William the Conqueror.

ORTON WATERVILLE

Orton Waterville takes its second name from its one-time feudal owners, the Watervilles, whose family owned the manors of Overton and Thorpe as tenants to the Abbots of Peterborough. The village sign stands at the junction of Oundle Road (A605) and Cherry Orton Road, at the entrance to the old village. It was erected in 1977 to commemorate the Queen's Silver Jubilee and is a simple stone plinth on which is a metal plate recording the event of the Silver Jubilee.

OUTWELL

Outwell and Upwell lie astride the Well Stream. Each is therefore partly in Norfolk and partly in the Isle of Ely. In the Middle Ages they were collectively known as 'Welle' or 'Welles' and today they are continuous, stretching about 4 miles along the old course of the Nene, and they are considered locally to be 'the longest village in England'.

After the Nene had been diverted, to the course it now follows, the Well Stream gradually became smaller and rather silted up. It is only since the 1960s that the river has been cleared and cleaned out and stocked with fish, the work having mainly been done by volunteers who formed the Well Creek Trust. The name of Outwell derives from the Anglo-Saxon word 'ut', meaning out, and thus a literal translation is 'the well lying just outside the village', or 'the outlying settlement by the spring'.

OUTWELL

Designed and made by the late Harry Carter of Swaffham, Outwell's village sign, which was unveiled by the Women's Institute in September 1977 to celebrate its Golden Jubilee, stands on the village green, formerly the site of the old canal.

On the north side is a picture of the 16th–century Beaupre Hall which was demolished in the 1960s. The Beaupre family acquired lands here from Edward VI. The oldest parts of the Hall, built of brick with stone dressings, dated from about 1500 and included much of the central block. On the south side, a loaded barge, perhaps carrying produce to Wisbech and then onto Lynn, is shown on the Well Creek, a navigable waterway, crossing over the Middle Level Main Drain at Mullicourt Aqueduct.

PARSON DROVE

Parson Drove lies 5 miles west of Wisbech near to the North Level Main Drain. Its name is thought to derive from the custom of a local parson, who lived in the neighbouring village of Leverington, walking along the mud road or 'drove' to take services in the village church.

Designed by a local resident and made by Tod Rayner of Lower Gresham, the village sign, which stands on the green facing the Village Hall at the crossroads, was unveiled in December 1977 to commemorate the Silver Jubilee of Queen Elizabeth II as shown by the crown, the letters ERII and the date 1977 which are painted on the sign.

Pepys stayed in the village on 17/18 September 1663 and described it as a heathen place, where he had to sleep in a cold, sad, stony chamber in a miserable inn. This inn was the Swan. On the green, near to the Swan Inn, is the old village lock-up or Cage, which later housed the village fire engine; today the building serves as the Village Hall. This building is depicted in the sign. In 1897, to commemorate Queen Victoria's Diamond Jubilee, a clock tower was built onto its roof. The clock faces are unusual in that letters, instead of numbers, are used which spell 'VR Sixty Years'.

Beneath this a cornucopia spills out the agricultural crops of the area. Among these crops is the woad plant with its bright yellow flowers and blue-green leaves from which the pigment woad was once made for dying cloth. In the past, Parson Drove was famous for its woad.

PEAKIRK

The small village of Peakirk lies approximately 7 miles northwest of Peterborough and is renowned for two very different things - the remarkable wall-paintings in the parish church and the Wildfowl Gardens on the back road to Deeping. The distinctive name Peakirk commemorates Saint Pega or Pea, a sister of Saint Guthlac, founder of Crowland Abbey. She is reported to have retired to the village after her brother's death where she formed a religious community, which was repeatedly destroyed and reformed. It was initially destroyed by the Danes in 870 then again in 1013 by which time it had become a hermitage. In 1048, having been restored for the 3rd time, it was made a dependency of Crowland Abbey. After the Conquest more substantial buildings took the place of the earlier wooden ones. Saint Pega's cell is alleged to have stood where today a modern house called the Hermitage stands. Saint Pega, who died in Rome in 716, where she had gone on a pilgrimage, is featured in the centre of the village sign.

In Roman times, Car Dyke - one of the original flood banks of East Anglia - passed through an osier bed at Peakirk. Now that same site, transformed by The Wildfowl Trust, has become an important centre for wildfowl, with a collection of 700 birds of 115 different kinds. The village sign's background depicts a pond and wildfowl representative of the Wildfowl & Wetlands Centre.

PERRY

Perry is situated off the B661, on the edge of Grafham Water, some 6 miles south-east of Huntingdon. It is a small parish established in 1982. At its northern end there is a bird sanctuary and nature reserve; whilst modern housing separates the lake from the Buckden to Great Staughton road. The village sign, which stands outside the Wheatsheaf Inn, was unveiled on 19 September 1986 by a local artist, Mr Thomas Gamble of Blythe Green who also designed and painted it.

The sign depicts sailing boats, trout and fishing flies which represent the village's connection with the water sports and activities of the Grafham Water Sailing Centre.

Representative of the farming community that surrounds Perry, the sign depicts a farm hand and a sheaf of corn; the latter also represents the village Public House, The Wheatsheaf Inn, which has a bar in the design of a boat. Finally, the area has much to offer, in terms of bird and wildlife, for the naturalist and country walker and this is represented, on the left-hand side of the sign, by the gentleman in country attire.

PONDERSBRIDGE

The present name of Pondersbridge has a shortened alias 'Pondsbridge', and is a post-drainage name given to a bridge over the Bevill's Leam, a cut short-circuiting the river Nene after Whittlesey Mere had been drained. The village stands in a bleak position right in the middle of fenland on the long straight fen road from Ramsey Heights to Whittlesey. Scattered over the district are the isolated fenland farms and drove ways. The hamlet contains a few cottages, a former vicarage and a yellow brick church dedicated to St Thomas, which was built in 1869. The church has a polygonal north west turret typical of High Victorian churches of this period. Pondersbridge was constituted an ecclesiastical parish in 1866. The village sign was erected to commemorate the Silver Jubilee of Queen Elizabeth II.

PYMOOR

Pymoor, 4 miles north-west of Ely on the B1411, is a small community running parallel with the east side of the New Bedford River. Designed by Tony Taylor and carved out of solid oak by Mr Ian Agrel, the village sign was unveiled on 28 May 1980.

Pymoor is the old spelling, in contrast to Pymore which has been adopted by the Post Office and used by them since 1974. Pymoor means 'flies over a bog' which does not sound very attractive but on the sign is a lovely dragonfly hovering on the marsh weeds, with a leaping fish and wildfowl which still abound at Pymoor. The windmill represents one of the many that were used for drainage of the fens. Pymoor used to have at least 2 windmills, one of which, in later years, was used to grind corn and as a bakery. Close to Pymoor is the Hundred Foot Pumping Engine which pumps water from the drain into the river. On that spot first stood a windmill, followed by a steam engine, a diesel engine and now one driven by electricity. The oak leaves in the corners represent the huge bog oaks which are still ploughed up today.

RAMSEY

Ramsey stands, equidistant between Huntingdon and Peterborough, on what was once an island in the fens and was the largest parish in the former county of Huntingdonshire. Nearly the whole of its 17,000 acres is rich fenland soil under cultivation; the principal crops being market garden produce, particularly potatoes, celery, carrots and sugar beet.

Much discussion has taken place over the derivation of the meaning of the name Ramsey. The ending '-ey' means either an actual island or a piece of firm ground surrounded by bog or marsh. Thus, in the Middle Ages Ramsey was said to be 'the island of branches', from the Latin word ramis, for 'the island is as it were hedged about by great trees'. Since Ramsey was a piece of dray ground in the midst of fen this seems most unlikely. Another argument said it was Raven's island, however, as ravens are even rarer than great trees at Ramsey, Raven or Hraefn must have been a personal name. Alternatively, it could have been the island where the hramsa, ransome or wild garlic, grows. The only agreement amongst experts is that Ramsey does not mean what might seem the most obvious explanation, namely the island of rams. Having said that, the village sign, which was erected in Spring 1978 by the Silver Jubilee Committee to Commemorate the Queen's Silver Jubilee, depicts a ram representative of Rams Isle. Also depicted on the sign are sugar beet, carrots and a tractor representative of the farming community associated with Ramsey. The sign stands in a garden of a private house at the edge of Bury Road just past the junction to Brands Close.

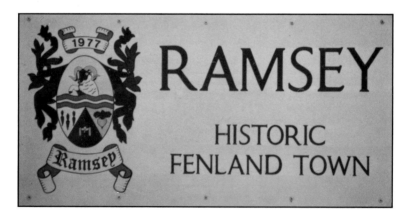

SAWTRY

Sawtry village sign was erected on The Green in the summer of 1985 to celebrate the 900th Anniversary of the Domesday Survey made by William the Conqueror and in which Sawtry is mentioned in 1085. Several drawings were submitted to the Parish Council showing a symbolic representation of Sawtry's history, location and character. The chosen design was made in the workshop of Mr Gowing, blacksmith of Soham. Sawtry used to be known as Saltreiam meaning 'landing place for sellers of salt', thus the centrepiece of the design is a hexagon of a salt crystal with a diagram of sodium and chlorine ions. Above the crystal is a medieval ship laden with salt. Either side of the ship are men unloading salt. In the middle of the crystal is All Saints' Crown representing the Parish of All Saints. Beneath the hexagon is the Star of David, for the Jewish name of Judith, with the initials SJ in the centre representing the Parish of Sawtry Judith, often wrongly referred to as Sawtry St Judith. Behind the salt crystal is a Stone Cross representing St Andrew's Parish. These three parishes were the original three "Sawtrys". Today, Sawtry All Saints forms the nucleus of the village, whereas all that remains of Sawtry St Andrews, on the eastern side of the A1(T), is the derelict churchyard with a few memorials and a cottage or two. The location of Sawtry St Judith was discovered from the analysis of aerial photographs and does not remain today.

The cattle, on the left-hand side of the sign's main panel, represent Bullock Road in contrast to the heavy lorries and car pictured on the right-hand side which represent the Great North Road, the A1(T). The 4 corners of the main panel, in the order top left-hand corner clockwise through to bottom left-hand corner, depict the crests of the Cavendish, Cromwell, Beaumes and Louthe families. Finally, either side of the name Satltreiam is depicted part of the heraldic device of Sawtry Abbey (bar gules or fretting). A goose and eels are also depicted.

STIBBINGTON

The village of Stibbington, whose name derives from the Anglo-Saxon personal name of Stybbinga, literally translated means 'town of Stybbings or sons of Stybba'. It was originally part of the Roman town of Durobrivae, and there are still Roman kilns in the corner of the field by a small council estate called Roman Drive.

Ermine Street, the forerunner of the Great North Road, the A1, linked London with roman fortresses at Lincoln and York. To guard the point where Ermine Street crossed the river Nene, a small 5–acre fort was built in the mid-first century AD at Water Newton, which stands on the south bank of the river Nene between Alwalton and Stibbington. A civilian settlement soon appeared at the gates of the Water Newton fort. The later parish boundary now separates the town of Durobrivae from the Water Newton fort; and the parish that contains the site of Durobrivae is called Chesterton, meaning the 'town' near the 'chester' or Roman town. The name Durobrivae, meaning 'the fort at the ford', comes from the Latin word duro meaning 'walled place' and from the Celtic word briva meaning 'bridge' The name was probably transferred from the Water Newton fort as the town walls were built late in the Roman period.

Stibbington village sign stands at the bottom of New Lane on the embankment with the A1(T) road. It was presented to the Parish by Wansford & Stibbington Women's Institute on 22 October 1988. The design features Stibbington church, which was drastically restored in 1848-9 when it lost its original shape and many interesting features were replaced by, in the words of the rebuilders, 'something better'.

In the foreground, are shown a river, stepping stones and a Roman soldier symbolic of Stibbington's Roman past and the fact that it was here that Ermine Street crossed the River Nene.

STILTON

Nearly 2000 years ago the Roman legions marched along Ermine Street on the road that was later to become one of Britain's busiest thoroughfares - the Great North Road. Along this route, now bypassed by the A1(T), is the village of Stilton. The name probably derives from the Anglo-Saxon word 'sticol' meaning both steep and rough as Stilton lies in a hollow, and would have had to be entered from either end down a steep incline. This translation is borne out by earlier recordings of the village name as Stiltone and Sticiltone.

Two hundred and fifty years ago, travellers were still using the same route stopping at the many posting houses in the village. In particular, the Angel Inn and Bell Inn are of note, the latter being famous because of its link with Stilton cheese. The Bell Inn is a fine building in Northamptonshire stone and was in existence in 1515, being rebuilt as it is now in 1642. It was later sub-divided into houses with the inn at one end. It was the enterprising 18th–century landlord, Cooper Thornhill, who put Stilton gastronomically on the map by popularising the eating of Stilton cheese. A local cheese had been sold in the village for some years and as sales increased by the early 1730s Cooper Thornhill was obtaining additional supplies from his sister-in-law in Leicestershire. It was this cheese sold exclusively to Cooper, much to the irritation of the landlord of the Angel, whose own cheese, locally made, could not compare, that put Stilton on the map.

The village sign, which was presented to the village by the Stilton Women's Institute to mark their Golden Jubilee in 1981, depicts the Bell Inn with a stagecoach and passengers.

SUTTON IN THE ISLE

South of Mepal, Sutton, whose name derives from 'southern farm', stands on a ridge of land above the fens, at the south–west edge of the Isle of Ely, along the ancient route from Ely to Huntingdon.

A top of the ridge, upon which the village stands, the parish church of St Andrew rises tall and dominates the skyline with its beautiful 14th–century tower. The church, which was built about 1370 in the time of Bishop Barnet, ranks as one of the finest in the county. The grand two-storeyed, vaulted south porch bears, on its bosses, the arms of Barnet and his successor, Thomas Arundel, Bishop of Ely at 21, Richard II's Chancellor, transferred to York in 1388, and who then helped Henry IV to power in the revolution of 1399. From the lofty nave rises the magnificent tower which has a large and smaller octagon on top of its three buttressed stages. Locally, it is known as the 'Pepperbox' and it contains a ring of old bells suspended on a 17th–century timber frame.

Sutton in the Isle village sign was erected in 1984 to celebrate the 60th anniversary of the village Women's Institute. The double-sided village sign depicts the church on both sides; on the one side a daylight scene is shown whilst on the reverse the church is outlined at dusk with a view of the fens.

THORNEY

Thorney was once called 'Ancarig' which means 'Isle of the Hermits'. Its present name derives from 'Isle of Thorns'. The village lies farthest west of the old Isle of Ely.

The village has 4 signs; a sign being located at each entrance to the village. The first two signs, at Whittlesey Road and Station Road, were unveiled on 15th September 1980. The other two signs were unveiled a week later. The four signs were bought by the Thorney Appeals Committee, a small local fundraising committee.

Two of the signs depict Thorney Abbey, which was founded in the 7th century, with a monk standing on either side.

THORNEY

The other two signs depict the Tank Yard Building in Thorney. Thorney is the only parish in the Isle of Ely to have been the sole property for a long period of an occasionally resident landlord, the successive Earls and Dukes of Bedford, who were responsible for much of the fen drainage. The Bedford coat of arms is shown on the post below the village name. The 19th–century Duke of Bedford planned an estate village providing good accommodation for the workers. Part of the then modern improvements was a strange building in Tank yard which was five storeys in height. This unique building was built in 1855 as a water pumping station for the district. On the top floor was a water tank which provided water for the community. Below this was a chamber which received the village sewage en route for disposal. After being derelict for many years, in 1981 part of the building was converted into a village hall, parish council chamber, Heritage Centre and a few small industrial units at the rear.

THORNHAUGH

Thornhaugh, near to Wittering airfield, is a small village situated to the west of the A1 trunk road. The houses are arranged up the western slope of the hill along its only main street.

Thornhaugh is remembered for 3 tragedies which took place within its confines. Half-covered by the organ in the church is a stone commemorating Ovenus Cambridge, accidentally shot by his manservant in mistake for a deer in 1672; over the west door is a memorial to a little boy, George Gaskell, killed during rabbit shooting in 1810; and on the south wall a tablet records the drowning of Mrs Charlotte Wing, wife of the rector, and their daughter Ellen, while boating on the river Nene in 1838.

The village sign, presented by Stibbington and Wansford Women's Institute in 1985, is a simple name plate mounted upon a large stone set off to the side of the road in the middle of the village.

TYDD ST GILES

Tydd St Giles is the Isle of Ely's northernmost village, situated 6 miles north of Wisbech, and overlooks the Lincolnshire boundary. The name derives from the Anglo-Saxon personal name of Tidi or Tidda as evidenced by other town names of Tidmarsh, Tidworth and Tiddington.

Designed by Mr Norman Pentelow, the village sign was unveiled on Sunday 4 June 1978 by Tydd St Giles Women's Institute on the occasion of its 50th anniversary.

The sign depicts the beautiful 12th–century village church, which is built of Barnack stone. It is unusual in that the tower stands apart some 50 feet from the main building and it is one of three in the area of similar design. The sign also depicts St Giles, the patron saint of the church and whom the village is named after. Tydd St Giles is set right in the north east of Cambridgeshire and is, and always has been, engaged mainly in agriculture. The soil is highly fertile and much given over to orchards and market gardens. Thus, a strawberry punnet, a sheaf of corn, and pitchfork represent the village's link with agriculture. Allied to agriculture in years past, Tydd had its own wheelwright and this man's daughter carried on the trade, after he died, until she was quite elderly. Thus, a cart wheel is depicted to represent what is thought to have been the only known lady wheelwright in the county. Finally, the anvil represents the village's long association with blacksmiths. Two brothers were the last in a 200 year line of smiths. The last one died in 1983, and with his death the blacksmith's business disappeared.

UPTON

This tiny village, near the top of Stangate Hill on the A1 trunk road, is built around the meeting place of roads from the Ermine Street in the east, Hamerton in the west, and along Coppingford Lane from Coppingford on the north-east. The place-name of Upton suggests that the parish was once within the soke of Alconbury, since the modern village stands on the hillside, overlooking the estate centre of Alconbury a short distance to the south - hence 'Upton'.

Designed by Brian Fountain, artwork by Catherine Baker and made by Glyn Mould of Lilford Park, Upton village sign, which was unveiled 8th July 1989, stands on the edge of the village pond at the junction to Glebe Farm and opposite the village's Early English church of St Margaret.

Either side of the village name, the sign depicts 2 shields, each of which is of a family associated with the history of the village. The undertenant of Upton in 1086 was Fulk de Beville, and his descendant Richard de Beville died circa 1238 leaving three daughters and co-heirs, namely, Alice the wife of David de Malpas otherwise the Bastard, Cecily the wife of Robert de Sibthorpe, and Margery the wife of Geoffrey de Raund. The Beville shield is depicted at the far right of the sign.

The most important pourparty in Upton, which included the church advowson, was that of Beville's third daughter, Margery, who married Geoffrey de Raund. Geoffrey presented to the church in 1252, but shortly afterwards his interest had passed to Sir Guy Gobaud of Newball in Stainton, Lincolnshire, who succeeded his father, John Gobaud, in 1258 and presented to the church in Upton in 1273. The Gobaud shield is depicted at the far left of the sign.

John, son of Sir Guy Gobaud, married Margaret, who after his death married Edmund de Colville of Castle Bytham in Lincolnshire and in 1310 presented to the church as Margaret de Colville widow of John Gobaud. Therefore, the Colville shield is depicted as the second shield from the right.

By the middle of the 15th century all the manors and pourparties of manors in Upton and Coppingford had passed into the hands of Richard Sapcote; the manor of Upton then descended with the Sapcotes of Elton until 1600. Thus, the final shield, displayed second from left, on the village sign is that of the Sapcote family.

Also depicted in the sign is a stagecoach as Upton used to be on the route of the London-York stagecoach run. In the background is the church of St Margaret, which was mentioned in the Domesday Book, however, the church has over the centuries undergone much restoration, and the earliest parts now in existence are the 12th–century south doorway and font.

UPWELL

Upwell, whose name means 'upper well', and the village of Outwell adjoin each other and from end to end are about 4 miles in length. Upwell is partly in Cambridgeshire and partly in Norfolk, the boundary being the ancient Welle stream.

The village sign, which stands eleven feet high on the Norfolk side of Church Bridge, was unveiled on 3 November 1979 by St Peter's Wives Group.

One side of the sign depicts St Peter's Church, built of Barnack stone and dating from the 13th century, which is in Norfolk and resembles a cathedral in miniature. Above the church are depicted the three fishes and sheaf of corn from the Upwell crest. The other side features the old 'Upwell Strawberry Tram', a small train which ran along the main road between Wisbech and Upwell until the 1940s and which was the main way of transporting the soft fruits in the season. On both sides are reminders of eel fishing which was once one of the main industries of the village.

UPWOOD

Upwood is a small attractive village which has managed to preserve its identity, possibly because, long ago, it seems to have been bypassed by the road to Ramsey. Upwood appears in the chronicles of Ramsey Abbey as the home of its founder Earl Ailwine. It had been given to Ailwine with the fisheries of the neighbouring streams by King Edgar. Ailwine had a hall here and often stayed to indulge in hunting and hawking and died there in 992.

Designed by Michael Gillespie and made by blacksmith Richard Gowing, the village sign was erected on the Huntingdon Road opposite the turning to Church Lane by the people of Upwood to commemorate the wedding of HRH Prince of Wales and Lady Diana Spencer in 1981. The sign symbolises the name of Upwood and its history from the time of the Saxon Earl Ailwine, who is symbolically depicted holding the crossed keys of St Peter, to whom the village church is dedicated, through to modern times.

Place names such as Upwood, Wood Walton, Woodhurst and Oldhurst suggest the presence of extensive forest, as does the name for the Anglo-Saxon hundred which covered this area of Huntingdonshire (Hurstingstone comes from the word 'Hurstingas', meaning 'forest dwellers'). The area probably reverted to forest during the early Anglo-Saxon era. Representative of this close association with the forest, the village sign depicts a wood on the bank of a river.

The village church of St Peter is depicted top right; nothing remains of the church mentioned in the Domesday Survey, which was probably built of timber, but about the year 1100 a stone church, consisting of a chancel and an aisle-less nave, was built, of which the chancel arch and part of the north wall of the nave remain.

WARBOYS

Warboys is a typical fenland village, standing on a high ridge with extensive views towards Chatteris and beyond. It is in two distinct parts, the older congregated near the church and former rectory and the more recent along the wide High Street to the east and at Mill End, where 2 windmills used to stand. Designed and made by the late Harry Carter of Swaffham, Warboys village sign, which was erected in 1981 to commemorate the wedding of Prince Charles to Lady Diana Spencer on the 29 July 1981, stands at the head of the 'Weir' (the village pond) at the junction of High Street and Mill Green.

On each side of the post are two witches in wrought ironwork in recognition of the notorious Witches of Warboys. The story of why 3 innocent people were done to death, on what was really a trumped up charge, occupies a prominent place in the sordid history of witchcraft, believed in by both high and low in the 16th century, which did not die out until the beginning of the 19th century. Three respectable people, John Samwell, his aged wife Agnes and their daughter Ann were tried and convicted at Huntingdon Assizes on 4th April 1593 of bewitching the 5 daughters of Robert Throgmorton Esquire of the Manor House, seven of his servants, Lady Cromwell, wife of Sir Henry Cromwell, and the gaoler's man, a 'crime' for which they were condemned to death and subsequently hanged. It is claimed in some accounts that they were the last in the country to be hanged for such practice. The father and daughter maintained their innocence to the end but Mrs Samwell finally 'confessed' after continuous interrogation and pressure. The full story is related in 'Legends of Huntingdonshire'. By law, Sir Henry Cromwell was entitled to the possessions of the victims but he must have had scruples for on September 28 the same year he gave the £40, the value of the estate, to provide for a lecturer from Queen's College, Cambridge, to preach in All Saints Church Huntingdon and 'to inveigh and preach against sorcery' each Lady Day. The lecturer was to receive 40 shillings but had to distribute 10 shillings to the poor. The 'Witches' Sermon' as it was called, continued to be preached until 1814 when it was tacitly discontinued.

The painted artwork of the double-sided sign depicts on the one side the earlier main occupations of the inhabitants of the parish, that is a horse and plough for agriculture and the Warboys Brickworks, now discontinued, whose erstwhile chimneys were visible as far away as Chatteris. Below this side of the sign on the sign post is depicted the Mitre of Abbot De Warboys of Ramsey Abbey. On the other side of the post there is an illustration of the Norman Sanctuary door-knocker which was refixed to the north door of the chancel, when it was rebuilt in 1832, of St Mary Magdalene Church. This, it is said, is one of only two of its type in the country, the other one being fixed on the outside of the main door of Durham Cathedral. It consists of a lion's face and ring formed by two winged dragons fighting.

The reverse side of the sign illustrates the Weir in which public baptisms by total immersion took place in early times, a windmill of which there were a few with Mill Green appropriately named, the White Hart outside which fox hunts used to meet and the Manor House, a 17th–century house, originally built by Sir John Leman, a local bigwig, which has Dutch-type shaped gables and which was once the home of the bewitched Throgmorton family.

The derivation of the name Warboys is of interest. It is a rare example of the partial translation of a Saxon name into Norman-French. In the Domesday Book it is spelt Wardebusc which is thought to mean 'look-out wood' (some say it is named after a former owner named Warde) which is appropriate as even today the wood can be seen from 7 miles away across the fens on the east. By 1150 the 'busc' part had been translated, by the Normans, into 'bois' the French word for a wood, but it was in the 17th century that the present misleading spelling of 'War Boys' was devised, and which some villagers believe has been responsible for the village having had a bad reputation in the past.

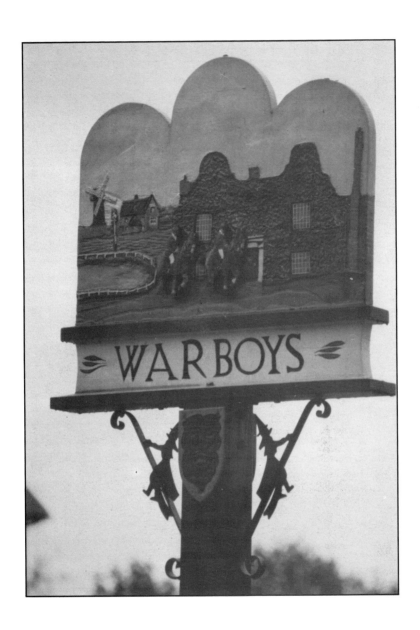

WENTWORTH

Wentworth village, whose name means 'winter homestead', is a very small village, which lies of the Sutton to Ely road. The village erected a very simple sign, made of wood and supported by two concrete posts, to commemorate the Queen's Silver Jubilee. Above the village name are the Jubilee dates and crossed keys representing St Peter's Church part of which dates back to Norman times. More notable, in the north wall of the sanctuary, is a bold early 12th–century carving of the patron, St Peter, with key and book and an abbreviated 'PETROS' inscribed behind his head.

WERRINGTON

Werrington, which was incorporated in 1929, was the most northerly village to be incorporated into the City of Peterborough. Werrington is the only one of the surrounding hamlets to have been included in the Domesday Book in 1086.

Erected by the village Women's Institute, the double-sided village sign is located on the green, opposite the Bluebell Public House, off Church Street Werrington road. One side depicts a ploughman and two–horse team with a mill in the background representative of the village's past association with agriculture. Most of Cambridgeshire's windmills have long ceased to operate or function, the majority having ceased work early in the present century. Today, most of the mills have disappeared or are derelict and Werrington's is no exception. In 1972 Werrington mill was recorded as a derelict grey brick (tarred) 5 storeyed tower in fair condition with flat roof.

The medieval scene, on the reverse side, represents Werrington Feast, an ancient village tradition, which used to take place on the first Sunday on or after 24th June, the Feast day of St John the Baptist.

WIMBLINGTON AND STONEA

The village of Wimblington, to the west of the A141, whose name means 'the farm of Winebeald's people', lies between Doddington and March. Designed and carved by Len Hopkins, Wimblington and Stonea village sign was unveiled on 5 June 1982 to commemorate the Royal Wedding and stands on a small green opposite the junctions of Addison Road, Norfolk Street and Church Street.

The double-sided sign symbolises the history of the village. The Heron, a native of the Fenland, symbolises the original marsh dweller; a keen-eyed expert angler adapted to his watery environment. The Shield portrays the network of Waterways which provide the Islands of fertile pastures and crops which now flourish. The 'Black Oaks' frequently unearthed are reminders of constant need to conserve the reclaimed land. Like ghostly oaks, history is always being unearthed. The Roman Villa at Stonea Grange is one relic of an early invader repelled by nature. The Norman Overlords found little welcome here. The Saxon hero, Hereward the Wake made good use of the natural defences of the Fen. Cromwell and his Ironsides made use of the natural fortifications in the area during the Civil War. Then came a more peaceful invader in the shape of the Dutchman who laced the Fen with drains and dykes which not only gave birth to the thriving farm industry but provided ample sport with rod and line.

On the reverse of the sign are carved, in 3 columns, Ten Horse Brasses, Heraldry of the Countryman, which tell the story of the village.

The Church and Chapel stand at opposite ends of the village, but are joined together in the service of God and the Community - 2nd from the top, middle column.

The School, founded in 1818, has tended the needs of generations. The Historical Pageant enacted by local children on the day that the sign was unveiled was a typical example of the School's many extra tutorial activities where parents and teachers work closely together - top, left-hand column.

The village still boasts several fine examples of the Thatchers' Art. Both reed and straw craftsmen hailed from the village. The durability of their work is a memorial to their skill and patience - middle, right-hand column.

In bygone days, sentinels in the shape of wind pumps kept watch on the water levels - now their electronic offspring maintain their unceasing vigil - bottom, left-hand column.

A perfect balance between land and water was achieved. 'Washlands' were created to absorb excess water and when dry they provided rich pasture for fine cattle - bottom, right-hand column.

The tilling of the soil and transport of produce was the domain of the 'Heavy Horse' and locally bred Percheron and Shire. These fine animals were in great demand as draught horses for Coal cart and Brewers dray - bottom, middle column.

These horses kept the village Blacksmith busy at his forge and his skill is still evident in the wrought ironwork of the sign. The cobble stones at the base rang out to the sound of his steel wheel rims - middle, left-hand column.

Then came the 'Iron Horse'. The village Railway Line and Station now lie buried beneath the new motor way, it has joined the Roman Villa and the 'Oaks' in history - top, right-hand column.

The Horse and Train have been replaced by modern transport methods operated by contractors based in the village and the old thatched barns have been stepped aside for the sophisticated Grain Dryer - 3rd from top, middle column.

No longer is the Eel catchers' Glave deftly thrust into the reeds, but every year the Sportsmen of the Angling world do battle with the slippery denizens of the waterways. The spirit of the Heron still lives - top, middle column.

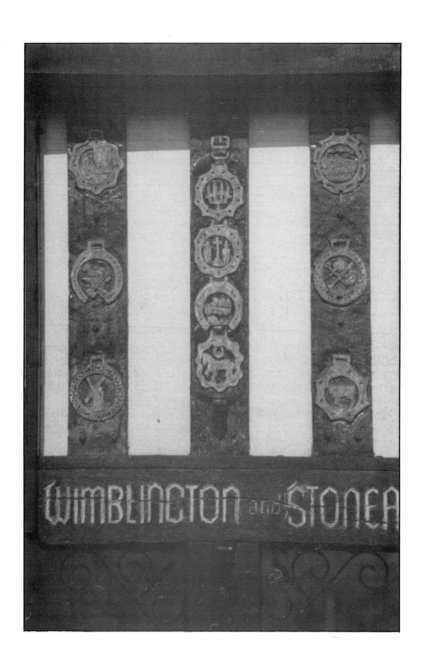

WITCHAM

Witcham, 5 miles west of Ely, perched on a low hill, is dominated by its church of St Martin, which dates back to the 13th century. The name of Witcham, formerly Wychham, is recorded in the Domesday Book as Wiceham, which is derived from the Anglo-Saxon name of Wica; hence a literal translation would be Wica's village.

Designed and carved by the late Harry Carter of Swaffham, Witcham village sign, which stands at the verge of the entrance road to the village, The Slade, was unveiled on 4 June 1980 and commemorates the Diamond Jubilee of Witcham Women's Institute.

One side of the sign depicts an early horse–drawn wagon loaded with hay or straw, representative of Witcham's farming connection, above which are two large wych elms symbolic of an alternative derivation of the village's name.

WITCHAM

The reverse side shows two gentlemen in early period dress standing in front of Witcham's own fire engine, which used to be filled with water by hand and then pulled to the fire by man power. The fire engine is now in Ely museum.

WITCHFORD

Witchford is located 3 miles west of Ely on the A142. In AD 607 St Augustine built a small church 'where the Wyche elm grows by the ford' and called it St Andrew's after his church in Rome. An RAF aerodrome was established at Witchford during the Second World War. The landing ground was on the plateau east of the village, in Ely.

Carved by Ian Algreve of Little Downham, the village sign, which was unveiled on 10 September 1983 to commemorate the Queen's Silver Jubilee, is located on the grass verge towards the Ely end of the village. A plaque, mounted with the sign, reads:

"In commemoration of the Silver Jubilee of Queen Elizabeth II 1952-77 and also the gallant airmen of Squadrons 115 and 196 stationed in the village during the Second World War".

The sign depicts the leaves and flowers of the Wytch Elm and a Ford through a small stream, representing the origins of the name Witchford (wych elm ford).

WOODHURST

Woodhurst, which is situated north of Huntingdonshire and St Ives is one of the finest examples of a ring village surviving in England. It is practically unaltered in shape since it was first founded in thick woodland over 2000 years ago. A ring village was the type of settlement made by clearing a stretch of woodland and surrounding the open space created by a road and then a strong fence or stockade to keep wild animals and intruders out. Today it is still possible to enter Woodhurst from either side and travel right around the village without leaving it. Hurst derives from the Anglo-Saxon word 'hyrstingas', meaning 'forest dwellers', a 'hyrst' being a copse or a wood.

The village was almost entirely destroyed by a fire in 1834, but a few 17th–century cottages remain. The Manor House stands at the north-east corner of the village. It is a large brick house with tiled roofs partly built in the 17th century and partly built in the 18th century. The Domesday Survey indicates two churches in St Ives, one probably being the chapel of Woodhurst.

Carved by Jack Clement, Woodhurst village sign, which stands on a small green opposite St John's Close and next to the church of St John the Baptist, was erected in March 1988 by the village Women's Institute. It depicts the village church which dates from the 12th century, pond and boxed water pump, which stands opposite the sign.